URBAN, SUBURBAN AND RURAL REGIONS IN THE USA

AMERICAN CULTURE FOR KIDS COMMUNITIES EDITION

3RD GRADE SOCIAL STUDIES

Speedy Publishing LLC

40 E. Main St. #1156

Newark, DE 19711

www.speedypublishing.com

Copyright 2017

In this book, we're going to talk about the three main types of populated regions in the United States—urban, suburban, and rural. So, let's get right to it!

Depending on where you live, you might have a huge community of people living close to you or you might live in an area where there aren't many other people. Some people use the word "city" to describe a populated area, but there are cities that don't have a large population at all, so that's not the best way to describe a densely packed area.

There are three terms that are generally used to describe how much population an area has and they are related to how many people are living close together. These terms are urban, suburban, and rural.

WHAT DOES URBAN MEAN?

Do you live in a region where there are lots of people living on a small area of land? Are there skyscrapers and tall office buildings near where you live? Are there commuter types of transportation like buses and trains that take people back and forth so that they use cars less?

Are there lots of cultural opportunities to go see a concert, a play, or the opera? Then, you might be living in an urban area. According to the United States census, if there are 1,000 people living in a square mile, then the region would be described as urban.

There are two general categories for urban areas in the United States:

- Urbanized Clusters have populations greater than 2,500 but less than 50,000

■ Urbanized Areas have a population of 50,000 or more with a density of 1,000 people or more living within one square mile

For example, New York City has the highest number of people packed into a small land area than any other United States city. For every square mile, there are more than 27,000 people!

Many urban areas are described as metropolitan areas, such as Greater New York. Sometimes two or more than two of these areas get so large that they are known as a "megalopolis." For example, the city of Boston in the state of Massachusetts continued to spread and spread until it got to Washington, D.C. The resulting megalopolis is sometimes referred to as BosWash or also described as the Northeast Corridor.

Not all countries define their urban areas in the same way. In Japan, where almost the entire country is densely populated, only areas that have 30,000 people or more are considered to be urban.

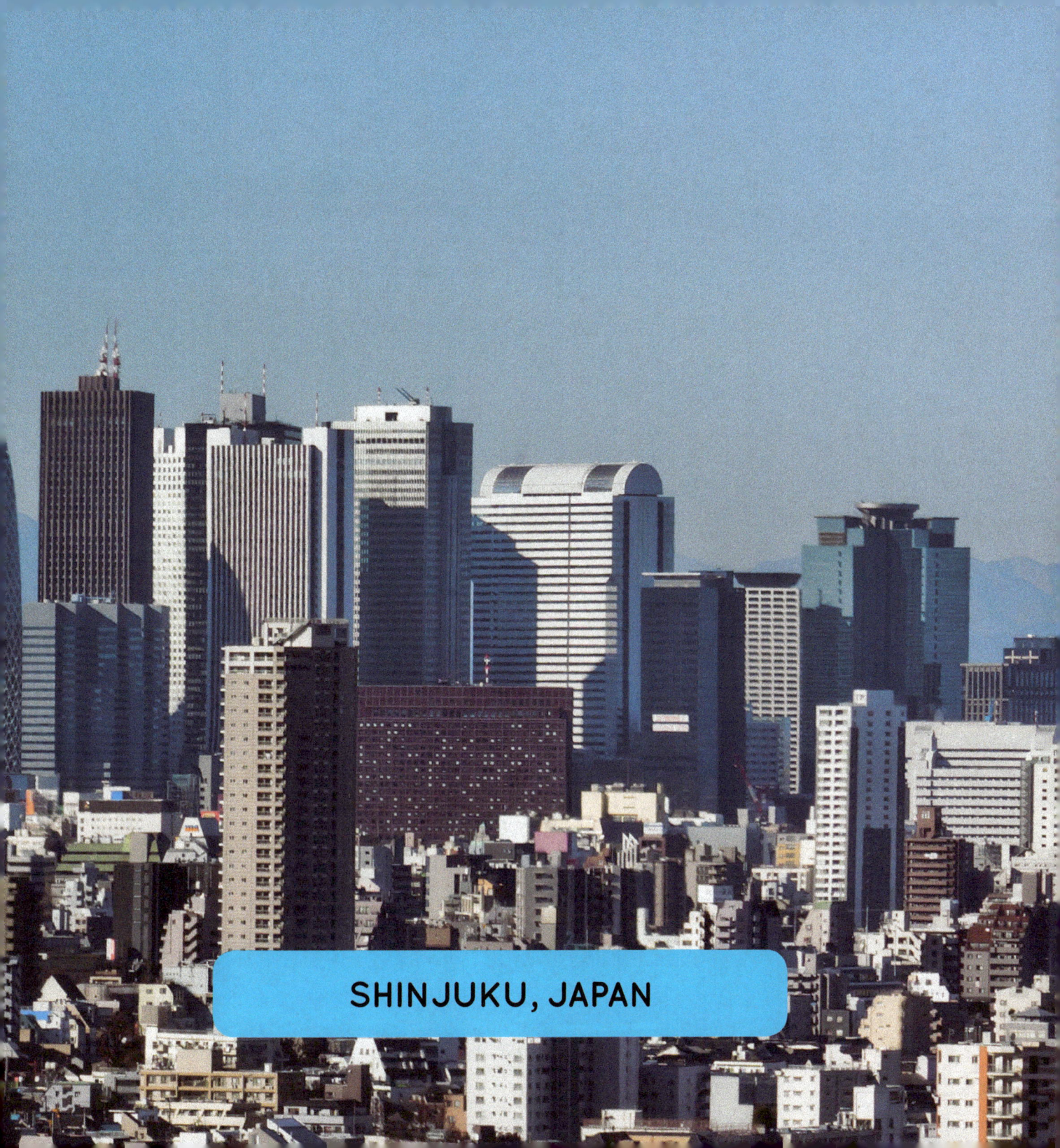
SHINJUKU, JAPAN

At one time, most of the people in the world lived in rural areas, but as of 2009 there have been more people living in urban areas than in the countryside.

One of the reasons that there has been a pattern of people moving from rural to urban areas is that not as many farming workers are needed. Improved technology has made it possible for less people to grow the food needed for a larger number of people. In general, urban areas also have more opportunities for jobs.

CHARACTERISTICS OF URBAN AREAS

There are a few common characteristics of most urban areas in the United States.

- The population is dense, at least 1,000 people per square mile.
- Most of the people who live there have jobs that are not related to farming.

There are lots of manmade structures, such as residences, office buildings, skyscrapers, shopping centers, highways, bridges, and commuter trains.

- There is usually a mix of offices, commercial buildings, and residences in close proximity to each other.
- There are lots of cultural activities.

- Pollution from the dense use of motor vehicles as well as from manufacturing facilities can sometimes be a problem.
- Green areas, such as parks, are generally planned and created instead of being part of the natural landscape.

WHAT DOES SUBURBAN MEAN?

Imagine that you are standing in the middle of a big city. It's an urban area with lots of traffic and people walking everywhere. Then, you get into your car and start to drive out of the city limits. On a map, if you drew a circle around the city as you drive further and further out, you will almost always come to a suburban area, sometimes called the suburbs or "the burbs" for short. These areas are usually primarily residences, but they are not as densely packed as housing in the city is.

Beginning in the late 1800s, many Americans began to move to the suburbs.

WALLSTREET, 1800'S

Innovations in transportation made it possible for them to commute from their residences to jobs in the city.

BELFAST, 1800'S

When World War II ended, the United States government offered special home loan programs to soldiers returning from the war. This spurred the growth of single-family homes in suburban areas across the United States.

SAN FANCISCO, 1945

In 1956, the Congress passed the Highway Act, which increased the system of interstate roads across the country by over 40,000 miles. This occurred during the Cold War with the Soviet Union. The original reason was so that there would be ways for people to escape in case there was a nuclear attack on a major American city.

The Cold War eventually came to a close but the suburbs continued to increase. In fact, as suburban areas keep getting larger and larger and spreading out more and more, over 2 million acres of the natural landscape, either farmland or wilderness, are lost to housing developments every year.

FARMLANDS TURNED INTO SUBURBS

CHARACTERISTICS OF SUBURBAN AREAS

Here are a few common characteristics of suburban areas in the United States:

- Suburban areas have less population density than urban areas.
- Suburbs have lots of single-family homes with much more space around them than residences in urban areas.

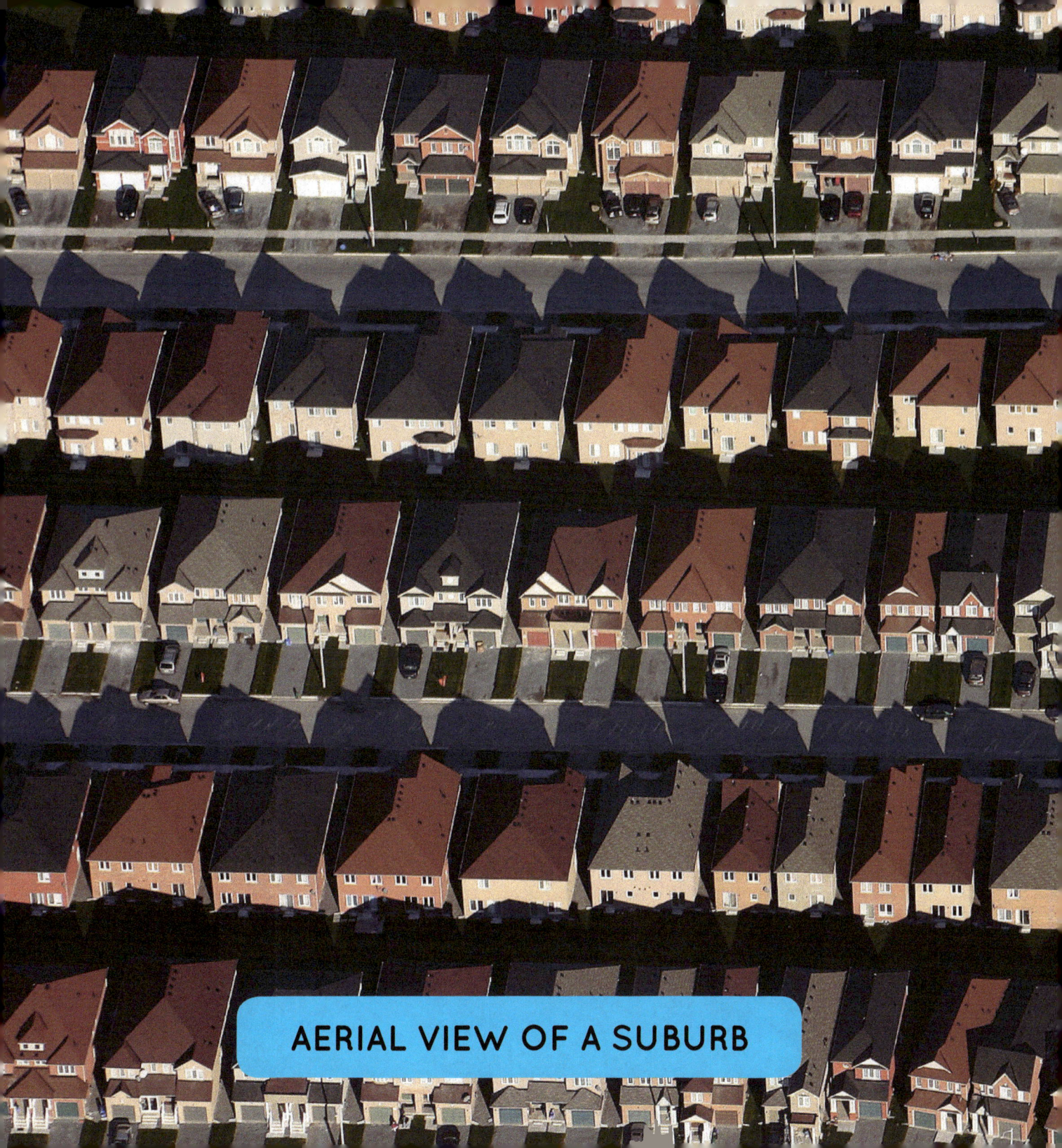
AERIAL VIEW OF A SUBURB

- The homes in suburban areas are usually larger in square foot size than urban dwellings.
- Suburbs have more open spaces and more planned parks than urban areas generally have.

- Most of the buildings in the suburbs are shops, services, schools, and residences.
- People sometimes like living in the suburbs to escape the traffic, pollution, or noise of a busy urban area.

WHAT IS SMART GROWTH?

Urban planners work to create "smart growth" of urban areas and to prevent too much suburban sprawl. There are several factors that contribute to smart growth of urban areas:

■ City planners develop neighborhoods that are less dependent on driving and easier for walking.

Instead of using farmland or open areas of land, urban planners are reclaiming rundown urban areas and rebuilding there.

New communities that are planned today have large areas of green space that isn't taken up by buildings.

■ Some states have passed legislature that prevents suburbs extending from their urban areas from getting too spread out. They limit the amount of land that housing developers can use.

■ More parks and more trees are being added to older neighborhoods in urban areas.

■ Many urban areas use drainage pipes to take away excess water, but new urban communities are developing manmade wetlands to handle the runoff from storms so that city streets don't get flooded.

WHAT DOES RURAL MEAN?

Rural areas don't have many people. Let's imagine once again that you've traveled from the core of a big city and now you've driven out of the urban area and you come to rows and rows of larger homes on plots of grassy land.

Then, as you continue to drive away from the city center and past the suburban area, you notice that the houses are appearing less and less. Instead, what you see is acres of rolling or flat farmland. Sometimes there are just plains or grasslands with a few isolated farms.

You've reached the rural region. The few people who live there are usually involved in farming or ranching.

In order for them to buy things, they have to drive into town. Their towns or cities are not usually very populated.

CHARACTERISTICS OF RURAL AREAS

Here are some of the major characteristics of rural areas:

- The population in most rural areas isn't as diverse as in urban areas. This just means that people in the country generally look similar in the way they dress and act.
- There is less population density in rural areas than in urban or suburban areas.

- The social life in the area is based on simple activities.
- The community is often very close-knit. People help each other in times of need.
- There's a lot of open space in rural communities and usually much less pollution.

THE US COMMUNITIES

Urban areas are very densely populated. In the United States, to be classified as an urban area, a region should have at least 1,000 people per square mile. Suburban areas are less densely populated than urban areas and consist of neighborhoods that are mostly residences, stores, schools, and services.

Many people drive or take other forms of transportation to work in the city. Rural areas are farms or wide-open wilderness areas. Less people live in these areas and there isn't much public transportation since there aren't enough people there to use it. There are some advantages and some disadvantages to every type of community.

Awesome! Now that you've read about urban, suburban, and rural areas of the United States, you may want to read about United States history in the Baby Professor book U.S. History 1820-1850 – Historical Timelines for Kids | American Historian Guide for Children.

Visit

BABY PROFESSOR
EDUCATION KIDS

www.BabyProfessorBooks.com

to download Free Baby Professor eBooks
and view our catalog of new and exciting
Children's Books

9 798869 401311